MW01134950

TRADITIONS AND CELEBRATIONS

GROUNDHOG DAY

DISCARD

North Richland Hills Public Library

by Sharon Katz Cooper

PEBBLE
a capstone imprint

Pebble Explore is published by Pebble, an imprint of Capstone.
1710 Roe Crest Drive
North Mankato, Minnesota 56003
www.capstonepub.com

Copyright © 2021 by Capstone. All rights reserved. No part of this publication may be reproduced in whole or in part, or stored on a retrieval system, or transmitted in any form or by any means, electronic, mechanical, photocopying, recording, or otherwise, without written permission of the publisher.

Library of Congress Cataloging-in-Publication Data is available on the Library of Congress website.
ISBN: 978-1-9771-3187-4 (library binding)
ISBN: 978-1-9771-3289-5 (paperback)
ISBN: 978-1-9771-5431-6 (ebook PDF)

Summary: Groundhog Day puts weather prediction in the paws of a rodent! Learn how people in the United States and elsewhere celebrate the day.

Image Credits
Alamy/Marshall Ikonography, 25; Associate Press/Craig Schreiner/Wisconsin State Journal, 22; Getty Images: Chris Hondros/Staff, 11, Jeff Swensen/Stringer, 12, 17, KAREN BLEIER/Staff, 23, Mark Wilson/Staff, 19; Newscom: ALAN FREED/REUTERS, 13, Christina Horsten/dap/picture-alliance, 14, 15, Margo Reed/TNS, 29; Shutterstock: Alan Freed, 7, Brian E Kushner, 5, Debbie Steinhausser, 26, Fiona M. Donnelly, 8, Isabel Eve, 21, Mark Van Scyoc, 6, 9, Mikhail Semenov, cover, 1, Rido, 27, Shelli Jensen, 28

Artistic elements: Shutterstock/Rafal Kulik

Editorial Credits
Editors: Jill Kalz and Julie Gassman; Designer: Juliette Peters; Media Researcher: Kelly Garvin; Production Specialist: Spencer Rosio

All internet sites appearing in back matter were available and accurate when this book was sent to press.

TABLE OF CONTENTS

Words in **bold** are in the glossary.

WHAT IS GROUNDHOG DAY?

Groundhog Day is an American **tradition**. It is **celebrated** on February 2. The biggest celebration takes place in Punxsutawney, Pennsylvania. A groundhog named Phil is the star.

Phil has a tradition. If he sees his shadow, there will be six more weeks of winter. What if the day is cloudy? Phil does not see his shadow. Then spring will come early. Phil is a weatherman groundhog!

PUNXSUTAWNEY PHIL

Groundhog Day began in Pennsylvania. The first Groundhog Day was in 1887. It happened at Gobbler's Knob. This is a small hill in Punxsutawney.

A sign marks the entrance to Gobbler's Knob.

Punxsutawney Phil

The Punxsutawney Groundhog Club led the way. They said their groundhog was the only one that could **predict** the **weather**. His name was Phil. Every groundhog since then has also been named Phil!

Groundhogs are brown, furry animals. They are about the size of a small dog. They eat berries, vegetables, and bugs. Groundhogs are also called woodchucks.

Phil lives in a special home at the library in Punxsutawney. You can visit him all year round.

Phil's home at the library

There are glass walls so you can watch him. You will likely find Phil eating or playing. Or he might be sleeping.

GROUNDHOG DAY IN PENNSYLVANIA

Every year, thousands of people come to Gobbler's Knob for Groundhog Day. The Groundhog Club holds three days of parties.

There are shows and activities for children. The club leads a big **ceremony**. Many news reporters come to find out what Phil will say.

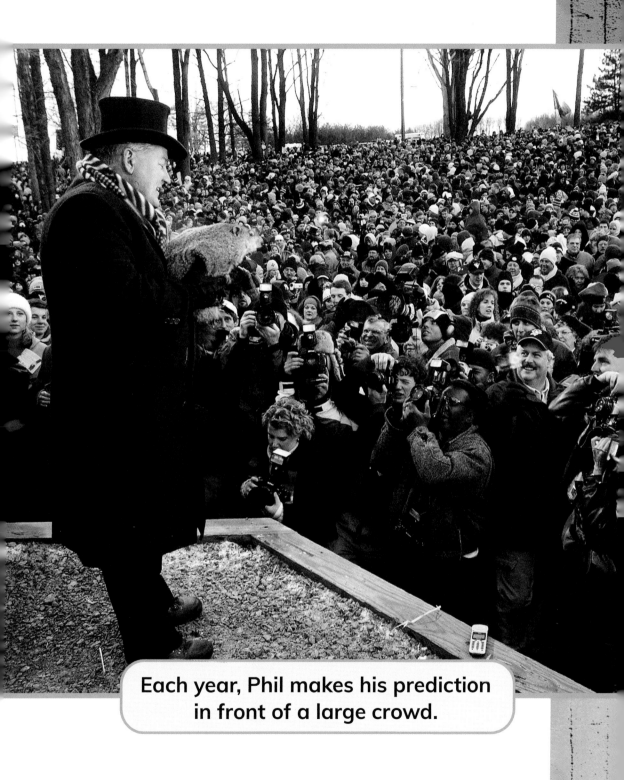

Each year, Phil makes his prediction in front of a large crowd.

The ceremony is shown on TV. It is even **live-streamed** on the internet. Phil's weather **prediction** is shared around the country.

A member of the Groundhog Club reads Phil's prediction to the crowd.

Phil is usually wrong! He gets it right less than half the time. Punxsutawney still calls itself the "weather capital of the world."

OTHER EVENTS

There are many fun things to do around Gobbler's Knob during the Groundhog celebration. You can walk along the Gobbler's Knob trail. You'll see metal art. It was made by students at a nearby school.

There are also signs along the trail. These signs tell visitors about Groundhog Day. There are colorful **sculptures** of Phil all around town.

Fireworks thrill the crowd before the groundhog ceremony. They begin at 6:30 in the morning! It is still dark then.

Children enjoy special stories and crafts. You can decorate a cookie or a top hat. You can watch wood carving and funny shows.

In the evening, grown-ups go to the Groundhog Ball. People dress up. They drink and eat. They dance to live music.

You can watch ice carving during Groundhog Day. Ice carvers use chainsaws to shape blocks of ice. They wear safety goggles and gloves. Ice chips spray in all directions! Soon the ice block is the right size and shape. Then they use smaller tools.

Carvers make a snowflake for six more weeks of winter. They carve flowers for an early spring. To finish their sculptures, they use a torch. The fire melts a tiny bit of the ice. This makes the sculpture look shiny.

A corn hole **tournament** is a popular part of the day. Twelve teams sign up to play each other. They play outside. Teams throw bean bags toward boards on the ground. They try to get the bags into small holes.

The winner of each round moves on to play another one. The losing team is out. The last team left is the winner!

GROUNDHOG DAY IN OTHER CITIES

Other cities in the U.S. also celebrate Groundhog Day. Sun Prairie, Wisconsin, says it is the Groundhog Capital of the World. Jimmy is the groundhog in Sun Prairie. People get together in the town square. Jimmy gives his weather prediction at sunrise.

Jimmy

Potomac Phil

Another celebration takes place in Washington, D.C. Potomac Phil is the star there. He is not alive. He is a stuffed groundhog. He predicts the weather. He also predicts some national news. People think it is a funny joke.

Cities in Canada also celebrate Groundhog Day on February 2. The most famous groundhog in Canada is Wiarton Willie. He lives in a house in Wiarton, Ontario.

The people of Wiarton wake him up to make his prediction. Then people celebrate with a parade. They also play hockey. They hold dances. They eat pancakes at a big breakfast!

Other cities in Canada have Balzac Billy, Brandon Bob, and Winnipeg Willow. These groundhogs share their own weather predictions.

A stone sculpture of Willie stands in Wiarton, Ontario.

AT SCHOOL

Kids celebrate Groundhog Day at school in many ways. Do you like to learn about animals? Your teacher might help you learn what groundhogs eat. Where do they live? When do they have babies?

Before February 2, you might make a chart of predictions. What will the groundhog say? Will he see his shadow or not? You can learn about shadows and light. Can you see your own shadow? How does light help you see it?

The predictions made on Groundhog Day are just for fun. They are not based on science. But Groundhog Day is still a great day to learn about weather and **seasons**.

How long does winter last? When does it end? How do we know when spring has arrived? The seasons are different in different places. What is spring like where you live?

Next February, tune in to see what the groundhog has to say!

GLOSSARY

celebrate (SEL-uh-brayt)—to do something fun on a special day

ceremony (SER-uh-moh-nee)—special actions performed to mark an important event

live-stream (LYV-STREEM)—to show on the internet the moment it is happening in real life

predict (pri-DIKT)—to guess about what will happen in the future

prediction (pre-DIK-shuhn)—a guess about what will happen in the future

sculpture (SKULP-chur)—a work of art made out of clay or metal

season (SEE-zuhn)—each of four parts of the year with different weather and daylight hours

tournament (TORN-a-mint)—a competition between teams

tradition (tra-DIH-shuhn)—a custom, idea, or belief passed down through time

weather (WEH-thur)—what it is like in the air, like rainy, windy, cold, snowy

READ MORE

Gillespie, Katie. *Groundhog Day*. New York: Av2 by Weigl, 2018.

Grack, Rachel. *Groundhog Day*. Minneapolis: Bellwether Media, 2018.

Reader, Jack. *The Story Behind Groundhog Day*. New York: PowerKids Press, 2020.

INTERNET SITES

Groundhog: Burrow Mania!
kids.nationalgeographic.com/animals/mammals/groundhog/

Groundhog Day: All About the Holidays
wqed.pbslearningmedia.org/resource/83dfbd1c-ef5b-4925-a225-ff835bef4496/groundhog-day-all-about-the-holidays/#.Xopb0YhKhPY

The Punxsutawney Groundhog Club
groundhog.org/

INDEX